FIRST-PERSON STORIES OF THE CIVIL RIGHTS MOVEMENT

AF904410

BY TAMRA B. ORR

ROSEN PUBLISHING PRIMARY SOURCE LIBRARY

ROSEN PUBLISHING

Published in 2027 by The Rosen Publishing Group, Inc.
2544 Clinton Street, Buffalo, NY 14224

Copyright © 2027 by The Rosen Publishing Group, Inc.

All rights reserved. No part of this book may be reproduced in any form without permission in writing from the publisher, except by a reviewer.

Designer: Deanna Lepovich
Editor: Nicole Horning

Cataloging-in-Publication Data

Names: Orr, Tamra B.
Title: First-person stories of the Civil Rights Movement / Tamra B. Orr.
Description: Buffalo, NY : Rosen Publishing, 2027. | Series: The Rosen Publishing primary source library | Includes glossary and index.
Identifiers: ISBN 9781725342866 (pbk.) | ISBN 9781725342873 (library bound) | ISBN 9781725342880 (ebook)
Subjects: LCSH: Civil rights movements--United States--Juvenile literature. | African Americans--Civil rights--History--Juvenile literature. | African Americans--Social conditions--20th century--Juvenile literature. | United States--Race relations--History--20th century--Juvenile literature.
Classification: LCC E185.61 O77 2027 | DDC 323.0973--dc23

Some of the images in this book illustrate individuals who are models. The depictions do not imply actual situations or events.

Manufactured in the United States of America

CPSIA Compliance Information: Batch #CSRYA27. For further information, contact Rosen Publishing at 1-800-237-9932.

Find us on

CONTENTS

FOREWORD

History is so much more than just a boring collection of names and dates. It is a collection of stories—sometimes tragic stories, sometimes heroic stories, sometimes romantic stories, sometimes scary stories. And they're all stories of real people who lived real lives.

Those stories can get lost in the shuffle of memorizing battles, studying maps, and listing important court cases or rulers. That's why primary sources are so valuable. They remind us that historical events happened to and because of real people. Reading diaries, looking at photographs, and seeing newspaper articles are just some ways to make history feel personal through primary sources.

Another way is through watching or listening to interviews with people who lived through major historical events. That's what you're invited to do in this book—and all the books that are part of the *Rosen Publishing Primary Source Library*. Each chapter includes quotes from an interview with a real person who experienced a major historical event in a deeply personal way. You can also scan the QR code included at the beginning of each chapter to watch a video interview with the person featured in that chapter.

Created in partnership with Generations Broadcasting, the *Rosen Publishing Primary Source Library* was created to remind readers that there is power in sharing our stories. First-person stories make history come alive. And when history comes alive, we're better able to learn from it—and avoid the mistakes of the past.

The events you're living through today will be part of the next generation's history lessons. As you read and watch the stories collected here, think about what you want your story to be.

Note: More interviews about the topics featured in this series, as well as many other historical events, can be accessed via a subscription to Rosen Publishing's GBC Stories Database: rosendigital.com/GBCStories/.

HOW TO WATCH THE INTERVIEWS FEATURED IN THIS BOOK

- Use your phone's camera, and hold it over the QR code.
- Click the link that appears.
- Watch the video that pops up. If you would like to read a transcript of the interview while you watch, you can click on that option in the video screen's menu.

INTRODUCTION

Protesting is often in the news today, but it is far from a new concept. It is guaranteed by the U.S. Constitution's First Amendment to allow people to assemble or gather and express their views. Naturally, participants have to follow some rules: Permits are generally required, and violence has serious consequences.

History is full of protests, from 1773's Boston Tea Party to 2025's No Kings gatherings. The involvement and input of the people in important issues is essential.

While the timeline of the United States is rife with all kinds of protests, one protest movement that truly changed the course of history—and continues to influence our world today—is the civil rights movement. It had its earliest roots during the abolitionist movement before the start of the American Civil War (1861-1865), which worked to end the practice of enslavement. Although the war and all of the Constitutional amendments and actions that followed focused on creating equality and justice for Black Americans, they did not result in creating a truly just and equal society. Many times it felt like one step forward was quickly followed by two steps backward.

The first stirrings of the modern civil rights movement came in the early 1950s. What began as one Supreme Court decision—declaring segregated schools **unconstitutional**—transformed into a country-wide movement. It made people across the United States reexamine their attitudes and analyze their prejudices. It made them question their own behavior as well as that of their friends, family, neighbors, and political leaders. And it inspired many Americans to stand up and demand equality for people of all races.

As the 1950s gave way to the 1960s, the civil rights movement gained momentum. Peaceful protests and violent **confrontations** made national headlines and were often shown on televised news programs. As the stories of the inequality and racially-motivated violence that plagued Black Americans reached new audiences, calls for change increased. New leaders of the movement emerged, and major steps were taken toward a fairer and more equal future for all Americans, regardless of race.

In 1971, a group of religious leaders from a variety of churches joined the Tallahassee Civil Rights March in Florida.

Many believe we still have more work to do to carry on the legacy of the civil rights movement, and we can start by studying the history of this movement and the lessons it can teach us. As you explore this book, pay close attention to the first-person stories included in it. These stories invite us to remember that the civil rights movement was not about far-off concepts. It was about improving the lives of real people who faced real discrimination and injustice simply because they were born Black in the United States. When we listen to and read about the stories of these real people, history comes alive in a way that can inspire us all.

CHAPTER ONE

VIOLENCE IN THE SOUTH

Major moments in history don't happen in a vacuum. They can often be traced back to earlier events and actions in the past, and they then affect the future in unique ways. In the case of the civil rights movement, which technically began in the middle of the 20th century, the battle for equality was the result of decades—and even centuries—of earlier history.

The civil rights movement was a response to the way Black people were treated in the United States, and one cannot talk about this topic without discussing the history of enslavement in the country. From the earliest days of the American colonies, Africans were taken from their homes, endured horrible conditions on long journeys across the ocean, and were forced to work without pay for enslavers.

Although the practice of enslavement ended across the United States with the Union victory in the American Civil War, this did not mean Black Americans were suddenly seen and treated as equal to white Americans. Instead, they often faced discrimination and, in many parts of the country, brutal violence.

The stories of this brutal violence, especially the lynchings

Scan this QR code to watch Charlene discuss growing up in Oxford, Mississippi, and learning about the violence that was perpetrated against the Black community in her hometown.

This image from 1936 shows a flag being flown to call attention to the crisis of lynching in the United States. Lynching is a form of mob violence in which a group of people murder another, often by hanging. This kind of violence has commonly been directed at Black Americans througthout U.S. history.

of Black Americans, serve to remind us of why the civil rights movement was necessary. Charlene learned these stories from her mother, who experienced the constant threat of violence in her hometown of Oxford, Mississippi.

LIMITED POSTWAR PROGRESS

The story of the civil rights movement can be traced back to the time of enslavement. While many states began outlawing the practice in the 19th century, it took a civil war for the practice to be stopped entirely. Once the Confederacy lost the American Civil War in April 1865, enslavement was **abolished** throughout the country, and formerly enslaved people were now considered "free." However, being legally considered "free" is one thing; being able to survive is something else. Formerly enslaved people often had no money or jobs, little to no education, and no homes or property. Progress had been made, but it was far too limited and did not make life as a Black American much easier or better. For

A crowd of people and a Union band pose in Massachusetts during the American Civil War. A Black man is sitting in a wheelbarrow as an indication of honor.

FAST FACT

THE AMERICAN CIVIL WAR WAS FOUGHT FROM 1861 TO 1865 BETWEEN THE NORTH, CALLED THE UNION, AND THE SOUTH, CALLED THE CONFEDERACY. THE ISSUE OF SLAVERY WAS ONE OF THE DRIVING FORCES BEHIND THE CONFEDERACY'S SECESSION FROM THE UNITED STATES. THIS WAS BECAUSE THE UNPAID LABOR OF ENSLAVED PEOPLE WAS ESSENTIAL TO THE ECONOMY OF THE SOUTH.

that to happen, the country had to make bigger and more permanent changes.

ADDING AMENDMENTS

One of the biggest hurdles to changing the country was making its new principles permanent. To ensure that slavery was forever abolished, the 13th Amendment to the U.S. Constitution was **ratified**, which ended slavery and involuntary servitude, unless it was for punishment for a convicted crime.

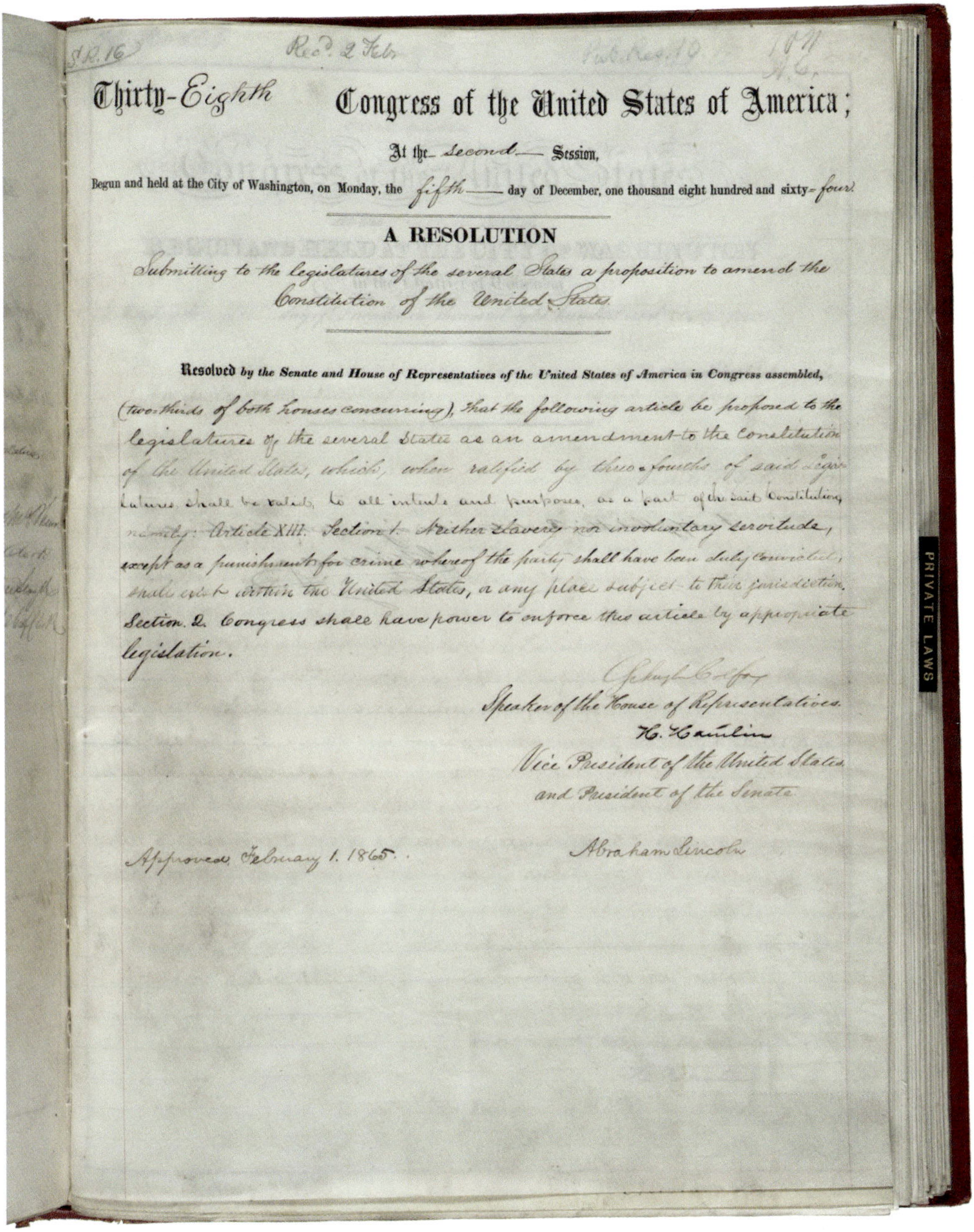

S.R. 16 Rec'd. 2 Feb Pub. Res. 10

Thirty-Eighth Congress of the United States of America;

At the second Session,

Begun and held at the City of Washington, on Monday, the fifth day of December, one thousand eight hundred and sixty-four.

A RESOLUTION

Submitting to the legislatures of the several States a proposition to amend the Constitution of the United States.

Resolved by the Senate and House of Representatives of the United States of America in Congress assembled, (two-thirds of both houses concurring), that the following article be proposed to the legislatures of the several States as an amendment to the Constitution of the United States, which, when ratified by three-fourths of said Legislatures shall be valid, to all intents and purposes, as a part of the said Constitution, namely: Article XIII. Section 1. Neither slavery nor involuntary servitude, except as a punishment for crime whereof the party shall have been duly convicted, shall exist within the United States, or any place subject to their jurisdiction. Section 2. Congress shall have power to enforce this article by appropriate legislation.

Schuyler Colfax
Speaker of the House of Representatives.

H. Hamlin
Vice President of the United States and President of the Senate

Approved, February 1. 1865.

Abraham Lincoln

PRIVATE LAWS

While the 13th Amendment (shown here as a proposed amendment) was ratified in 1865 by the required number of states, four states took much longer to ratify it. As reported on CBS News on February 18, 2013, Mississippi, due to a clerical order, did not officially ratify it until almost 150 years later.

FAST FACT

SUFFRAGIST SUSAN B. ANTHONY OPPOSED THE 15TH AMENDMENT. SHE DID NOT OPPOSE ALLOWING BLACK PEOPLE TO VOTE BUT WAS ANGRY THAT WOMEN DID NOT GET THAT SAME RIGHT.

In late 1864, President Abraham Lincoln began earnestly calling for support for this amendment. He put pressure on representatives to vote for it, stating that he expected representatives to acquire the votes needed to ratify the amendment. On January 31, 1865, the 13th Amendment was passed, and it was ratified on December 6. Unfortunately, Lincoln did not live long enough to see this amendment added to the Constitution. He was assassinated on April 14, 1865.

The same year the 13th Amendment was ratified, the 14th Amendment was proposed. It focused on who qualified as an American citizen. A person born in this country—regardless of skin color—was a citizen, according to this amendment. It was ratified in July 1868. It was followed, in 1870, by the 15th Amendment, which granted Black men the right to vote. All three of these amendments initiated some great strides in racial equality, but they were far from enough.

A HISTORY OF VIOLENCE

While Black Americans had legally been granted important rights following the Civil War and the abolition of slavery, life was still a struggle for many, especially those living in the South.

FAST FACT

IN THE 1930S, PHOTOGRAPHS OF PEOPLE WHO HAD BEEN LYNCHED WERE SOLD AS POSTCARDS, ESPECIALLY IN SOUTHERN STATES, EVEN THOUGH THERE WAS A 1908 BAN ON THIS TYPE OF MATERIAL.

Black people faced the constant threat of lynching. Thousands of these crimes were committed over nearly a century in southern states such as Mississippi, Georgia, Florida, and Texas. Defined as the public killing of a person without due process, this brutal form of murder resulted in the deaths of almost 5,000 people between 1882

Mobs such as the one shown here in 1933 were often the driving force behind the violent lynchings that plagued the South for many years following the Civil War.

and 1968. While the majority of them were Black, others were immigrants or white people who had helped Black people in some way.

The process of lynching began when a person was accused of a crime, ranging from vagrancy to sexual assault, or to just speaking in a "disrespectful manner" to a white person. Instead of getting a trial, violent mobs grabbed the person, and then often tortured them before hanging them or setting them on fire.

WHAT YOU'RE "SUPPOSED TO DO"

Charlene was a child growing up in Oxford, Mississippi, in the 1930s. Her mother ran a one-room schoolhouse. Charlene remembers Oxford as a "beautiful city". She stated in an interview that Oxford was designed in a large square:

THE BRUTAL MURDER OF EMMETT TILL

Spending the summer visiting relatives in Money, Mississippi, sounded like an adventure to 14-year-old Emmett Till. On a hot August day in 1955, he stopped by Bryant Grocery to buy some bubble gum. As he left, he called out, "Bye, baby!" to owner Carolyn Bryant.

Hours later, as Till was sleeping, he was hauled from his bed by Bryant's husband, Roy, and half-brother, J.W. Milan. The two white men beat him brutally, then shot him and tossed his body into the Tallahatchie River.

At the two men's trial, Carolyn testified that Till had grabbed her hand, pulled her behind the counter, and used vulgar language. (More than 60 years later, at age 82, she publicly admitted she had lied.) Roy and Milan were **acquitted** by an all-white, all-male jury.

Till's mother, Mamie Till-Mobley, did not accept her son's death quietly. She led a boycott of the Bryants' store until it was forced to close and the family moved out of state. Emmett's funeral drew more than 50,000 viewers and launched a strong response across the country. His death and the acquittal of his murderers helped spark the civil rights movement.

Only 100 days later, when Rosa Parks refused to abide by Montgomery city's bus segregation laws, she remembered the teen. Reverend Jesse Jackson said that Rosa initially thought about sitting in the back of the bus, but then remembered Emmett Till's murder and made her decision to defy the segregation laws. Dr. Martin Luther King Jr. also often referred to the horrible murder in his speeches and sermons.

This painting of Emmett Till was made by Dr. Lisa Whittington in 2012. It is titled *Emmett Till: How She Sent Him and How She Got Him Back.*

Shown here is Emmett Till's funeral. Mamie insisted on an open casket so that people could see what had been done to her son's body.

Billie Holiday was a jazz singer and songwriter. "Strange Fruit" was a song she popularized about lynchings and is often thought to be the first protest song of the civil rights movement.

FAST FACT

IN 1939, SINGER BILLIE HOLIDAY PERFORMED THE SONG "STRANGE FRUIT," WHICH WAS ABOUT LYNCHING, DESCRIBING BODIES HANGING FROM TREES. IN 1978, THE SONG WAS INDUCTED INTO THE GRAMMY HALL OF FAME.

The courthouse was in the middle of the square ... As you go around the square and you turn to the left, there was a store called the Golden Rule. That store was where my mother ... They would take my mother and all the Blacks by there to look at the heels of the

President Joe Biden and Vice President Kamala Harris are shown here at the signing of the Antilynching Act.

Black [people] that they had hung.

Based on both her memories and what she knew about history, she added, "From what I know from education now is [they did this] to let them know what we will do to you if you don't do what you are supposed to do."

FAST FACT

ON MARCH 29, 2022, PRESIDENT JOE BIDEN SIGNED THE EMMETT TILL ANTILYNCHING ACT INTO LAW. THIS MADE LYNCHING A FEDERAL **HATE CRIME**.

HOW YOU SEE HISTORY

1. Why do you think it took so long for the U.S. government to label lynching a hate crime?
2. Do you think the suffragists were reasonable for opposing the 15th Amendment? Why or why not?
3. Why do you think that Billie Holiday sang "Strange Fruit" at every one of her public concerts?

CHAPTER TWO

FIGHTING SEGREGATION

In addition to the constant threat of violence, Black Americans, especially those who lived in the South, faced other forms of mistreatment in first half of the 20th century. They included discrimination and segregation, and both were considered legal in many parts of the country at the time.

The practice of racial segregation often meant that Black Americans were given inferior goods and services simply because of the color of their skin. This had a lasting impact on the Black community, especially Black children who grew up during the time of legal segregation.

Tony was one of these children. His experiences in the segregated South mirror those of many young Black people at the time, and the effects of this period in U.S. history can still be felt today.

FEELING INFERIOR

During the era of legal segregation, Black people didn't have access to the same opportunities as white people. For example, Tony dreamed of joining the Air Force one day, but he did not believe it was remotely possible in the world he lived in.

In an interview, he said, "I didn't have the aspiration of

Scan this QR code to watch Tony discuss what his life was like during segregation and how he felt inferior simply for being Black.

Before desegregation, many cities had signs posted letting Black people know where they could and could not go.

actually being a pilot because I really didn't think I was smart enough to be one."

Tony grew up in the South and was surrounded by segregation, saying he was often "looked down upon" and it impacted his ability to realize what his potential might be. "Everything was segregated," he explained. "Water fountains, the lunch counters, the theaters, the movies, the churches, the cemeteries, hospitals, everything had signs on them—colored, white."

When he went to the movies, he said, Black people had to sit up in the balcony. They even had to buy their tickets separately and enter through a different door. "We naturally felt, at least I did, that I was really, really inferior," he said. He added he felt that white people must be better than he was.

Water coolers like this one were typically segregated. This was supposedly a way to offer "separate but equal" resources for Black and white Americans.

> **FAST FACT**
>
> IN 1963, ALABAMA GOVERNOR GEORGE WALLACE BRAGGED ABOUT HOW HE BLOCKED BLACK STUDENTS FROM GETTING INTO THE UNIVERSITY OF ALABAMA. HIS CAMPAIGN SPEECH WAS WRITTEN BY A KU KLUX KLAN MEMBER, AND IN THE SPEECH, HE SPOKE TO WANTING SEGREGATION NOW AND FOREVER.

"They gotta be smarter than me. They gotta be more intelligent. They gotta be wiser than me," Tony said.

Like so many people, Tony and his mother often stopped by their local Woolworth's store to eat. Tony recalled what it was like decades later. "I vividly remember ... having to go to the end of that counter to buy whatever we wanted. The hot dogs or the hamburgers or whatever and all these empty stools there," he described. "We couldn't sit in those empty stools ... we had to buy ours and walk away and go eat ... standing up in the store, basically." He and his mother would often take the food home or eat in their car instead.

Tony did end up joining the Air Force. He spent three years stationed in Germany, and it was an eye-opening experience for him. There was no segregation there.

When he returned to the United States, legal segregation was being slowly dismantled. However, Tony said, "Now it was under the table segregation. If you would go to a restaurant and you'd order something in particular off the menu, it wasn't uncommon

Woolworth's lunch counters played a significant role in the civil rights movement. In several cities around the world, Black people staged "sit-ins" at these lunch counters. They would sit at the counter peacefully and quietly. Their presence was a silent protest and it eventually led to Woolworth's desegregating.

for them to say, 'Well, right now we don't have that particular dish.' The message was, 'We don't want you in here.'"

"A FRIEND OF JUSTICE, A FOE OF INJUSTICE"

The National Association for the Advancement of Colored People (NAACP) was a major force in the civil rights movement, especially in its early years. The roots of this organization were in the fight against racially-motivated violence.

In August 1908, George Richardson and Joe James were sitting in a jail in Springfield, Illinois, accused of serious crimes. The sheriff, along with a local businessman, knew that these two Black men were in serious danger from the angry white people outside. They

NAACP leaders , including Thurgood Marshall (far right) show a poster speaking out against racism in Mississippi.

secretly moved them to a jail miles away for their safety. When the mob outside found this out, they were angry and wanted revenge. They headed into the Black neighborhoods, and white people damaged Black businesses and homes. Two men were lynched. The National Guard was called in to stop the violence.

FAST FACT

THE NAACP IS STILL VERY ACTIVE TODAY. IT HAS MORE THAN 2 MILLION MEMBERS AND MORE THAN 2,000 BRANCHES.

As word of this brutal attack spread across the country, more and more people were inspired to work for change. They gathered together—Black and white—and, on February 12, 1909, the NAACP was established. Their first motto was: "A friend of justice, a foe of injustice."

By 1919, the NAACP had 90,000 members and 300 branch offices. One of its goals was integrating public schools. However, it was a difficult battle.

EQUALITY AT SCHOOL

One of the biggest battles of the civil rights movement was the fight for all Black children to get the same education as white

Brown v. Board of Education **ruled that segregation was a violation of the 14th Amendment's Equal Protection Clause.**

While Black students had the right to a public education during the segregation era, they typically attended schools meant only for Black students. These were often in poor condition and resources were very limited.

FAST FACT

BROWN V. BOARD OF EDUCATION **DEMANDED THAT DESEGREGATION HAPPEN QUICKLY, BUT SOUTHERN STATES KEPT PUTTING OFF COMPLIANCE WITH THE LAW.**

students did. In 1954, the Supreme Court ruled in *Brown v. Board of Education* that segegating public schools based on race was unconstitutional.

It wasn't easy to integrate schools, though. In some states, especially in the South, there was violent resistance to desegregation. Black students were faced with white people who threatened to fire the students' parents from their jobs or **evict** them from their homes if they went to a "white" school. Some students were chased from school grounds and, if caught, were severely beaten.

Integrating public schools was a slow and often painful process. In September 1957, a group of nine teenagers became the first Black students to attend Little Rock Central High School in Little Rock, Arkansas. Known as the "Little Rock Nine", they were met by angry white families, and were spit on and

Robert Wagner, New York City's mayor in 1958, greets the first Black students to attend Little Rock Central High School in Arkansas. Unlike in some cities, these young people did not have National Guard support.

COURAGE IN MOTION

When six-year-old Ruby Bridges went to school on November 14, 1960, she had no idea that she was the center of a nationwide controversy. Because of her age, she was unaware of what was going in the world at that time, and her parents just told her that she was going to a new school and to behave.

Although public schools had been legally **mandated** to integrate Black students six years earlier, some were very slow to do so, especially in the South. It was no surprise that Ruby had to be escorted through the front doors of William Frantz Elementary School in Louisiana by her mother, Lucille, and several federal marshals. These men walked Ruby to school every single day of the school year.

As Ruby went up the steps to the doors, she had to walk past a crowd of angry people screaming and throwing eggs and tomatoes at her. As the first Black child to attend this all-white school, Ruby represented courage in motion. She later said that being an innocent child is what protected her at that time.

As Ruby walked down the hallway, every other first-grader walked out. Only one teacher was even willing to teach Ruby: Barbara Henry. Henry later said that for the entire school year, it was just her and Ruby and that neither of them missed a day of school at all.

Today, Ruby Bridges is an **activist** and author. She believes everyone has the power to take their abilities and use them for good in whatever way they can.

FAST FACT

IN HONOR OF RUBY'S COURAGE, SEVERAL SCHOOLS PARTICIPATE IN THE RUBY BRIDGES'S WALK TO SCHOOL DAY, HELD EACH YEAR IN MID-NOVEMBER. IN 2023, MORE THAN 650,000 STUDENTS AND TEACHERS TOOK PART.

threatened. President Dwight D. Eisenhower finally sent federal troops to the city to escort the determined teens inside.

The 1950s saw more changes than ever before in terms of civil rights, but America still had a long way to go. Fortunately, strong and passionate leaders were emerging, and they would help navigate the challenges to come.

Ruby Bridges did not truly understand that her first day of school was being watched around the country, but it was an image that spoke to many Americans.

HOW YOU SEE HISTORY

1. Do you think the "under the table segregation" Tony described still continues today?
2. Why do you think segregation made Black children like Tony feel inferior?
3. Why do you think schools in the South were allowed to take such a long time to desegregate?

CHAPTER THREE

THE FACES OF ACTIVISM

The civil rights movement was led by men and women whose purpose and passion inspired people of all races across the country. These leaders, especially Dr. Martin Luther King Jr., made a lasting impression on those who were fortunate enough to find themselves in their presence.

George was one such person who fondly remembered his meeting with Dr. King. As a white man living in Alabama during the time of segregation, George had a unique perspective on this chapter of the civil rights movement and his interactions with one of its most legendary figures.

"NEVER DID RAISE HIS ARM"

George was born in Montgomery, Alabama, in 1920. He worked for the state's Department of Industrial Relations during the era of segregation.

"We were operating under two laws," he explained in an interview, "state law, which says 'Thou shalt segregate,' and federal law ... which says, Thou shalt integrate.'"

George described going to his boss to ask what he should do: "I said, 'Sir, we going to have a real

Scan this QR code to watch George discuss what it was like to meet the legendary leader, Martin Luther King, Jr., when the battle for integration arrived in Montgomery, Alabama.

Dr. Martin Luther King Jr. gets a happy, warm greeting from his wife, Coretta Scott King, as he leaves court in March 1956. The two were married for 15 years.

crisis here before it's over with." He was told he was on his own to figure it out.

Soon after, Martin Luther King Jr. came to George's office. George had made sure not to segregate the waiting room. The two men spent 30 to 45 minutes together talking. George said he took King's application for work, honestly letting him know that the office rarely got any order for preachers, and especially not Black preachers. "But if we do, you will be the first to know," he reassured King. "We'll call and let you know."

George remembered King as a "very, very smart man" and a "very able speaker." In his interview, he sighed and added, "I thought that he was going to succeed. You see, he was an advocate of peaceful resistance. He never did raise his arm. None of his people raised their arm in resistance of what they were fighting against."

Rosa Parks was fingerprinted by a deputy sheriff after being arrested in 1956. She was arrested more than once.

ROSA PARKS

Another advocate for peaceful resistance was Rosa Parks. Looking back on it now, what she did on a Montgomery, Alabama, bus in 1955 might seem like a fairly tame form of rebellion. However, it was far from tame when Parks refused to stand up and give her seat to white passengers. Parks later said that while many people said she gave up her seat because she was tired, the reality was that she was tired of giving in to discriminatory laws.

FAST FACT

ALTHOUGH ROSA PARKS DID A GREAT DEAL FOR ADVANCING EQUALITY, HER LIFE AFTER THE BOYCOTT WAS DIFFICULT. SHE AND HER HUSBAND BOTH LOST THEIR JOBS, AND THEY RECEIVED DEATH THREATS. FINALLY, THEY MOVED OUT OF ALABAMA TO LIVE IN MICHIGAN.

On display at the Henry Ford Museum in Dearborn, Michigan, is the bus that Rosa Parks was on when she refused to stand up and started a major moment in the civil rights movement.

Parks was arrested by two police officers. Released on bail the next day, she was immediately encouraged by the head of the NAACP's Montgomery chapter, E. D. Nixon, to use her case to challenge the current segregation laws. One of the first steps the NAACP took was organizing a bus boycott to be held in the city on the day of her trial. They handed out thousands of flyers to tell others about the plan. From there, the news spread like wildfire. Leaders of Black churches announced the boycott. Newspapers published stories about it.

On the day of her trial, Parks was found guilty of violating segregation laws. She was given a suspended sentence and fined for court costs. That same day, 40,000 Black people did not take the bus. Instead, they walked to work and organized carpools, and Black taxi drivers in Montgomery reduced their fees for all Black passengers.

The boycott was just what the civil rights movement needed to gain attention. Instead of lasting one day, it went for more than a year. By the end of it, bus segregation was declared illegal in Alabama.

THE FREEDOM RIDERS

One lesson that all civil rights activists were learning was that just because a law was passed, it didn't mean that it was enforced

Outside of Anniston, Alabama, Black passengers watch as their Greyhound bus burns after being attacked.

throughout the nation, especially in the Southern states. Although the Supreme Court had ruled that segregation on public transport was unconstitutional in both *Morgan v. Virginia* (1946) and *Boynton v. Virginia* (1960), it didn't mean that Black people could safely board a bus.

The original "Freedom Riders," as they were called, were civil rights activists who rode interstate buses throughout the Southern states to call attention to this problem. John Lewis and Bernard Lafayette had previously challenged segregation by riding in the front of the bus and refusing to move. In 1961, they saw that the group Congress of Racial Equality (CORE) was sponsoring a longer bus ride through the South to challenge the laws. Lafayette wasn't allowed to participate in this ride, but Lewis joined.

In May 1961, the first ride left Washington, D.C., to go to New Orleans, Louisiana. The group faced some resistance in Virginia, but once they arrived in South Carolina, they started experiencing violence. John Lewis and another rider were both beaten, while another participant was arrested for using a whites-only restroom. The trip started attracting a lot of media attention. A few days after the incident in South Carolina, the group had dinner with Martin Luther King Jr. and other civil rights leaders. During the meeting, King told a reporter who was traveling with the group and covering their story that they would never make it through Alabama.

On May 14, the group arrived in Anniston, Alabama, where they were confronted by a violent mob of more than 100 people. Authorities in the area had given permission to the Ku Klux Klan (KKK) to attack the Freedom Riders without any repercussions. One bus was firebombed, and the passengers were forced into the mob. The violence continued once the group made it to Birmingham, where the police offered no protection. The violence drew national attention, but it also led CORE group member James Farmer to end the first Freedom Rides.

Between May and November 1961, more than 400 civil rights activists risked their lives in the first Freedom Rides. Martin Luther King Jr. gave his full support to their efforts.

FAST FACT

IN EARLY 1956, THE HOMES OF BOTH MARTIN LUTHER KING JR. AND E.D. NIXON WERE BOMBED. AFTER THE ATTACK, KING REASSURED FOLLOWERS THAT HE AND HIS FAMILY WERE NOT HURT AND TO BE CALM. HE ALSO TOLD THE CROWD THAT IF ANYTHING HAPPENED TO HIM, OTHER LEADERS WOULD TAKE HIS PLACE.

Martin Luther King Jr. would become one of the most powerful and influential leaders of the 1960s.

AN ADVOCATE OF PEACEFUL RESISTANCE

The Freedom Riders and boycotts after Parks's bus protest changed bus segregation laws in Alabama and served as a role model for the rest of the nation. Following Parks' original arrest, Black leaders in the state formed the Montgomery Improvement Association (MIA). They elected a young

MALCOLM X

Malcolm X, born Malcolm Little in Omaha, Nebraska, in 1925, was a man dedicated to fighting injustice. To the world, he was a vocal activist. To his four children, he was just "dad." His daughter Ilyasah didn't even know her dad was a civil rights icon until she was in school and had to study him in class. Malcolm X made sure his children knew how important love and compassion were. Later, in school, Ilyasah learned about racism and injustice and her dad's work to make the world a better place.

Malcolm X's approach to encouraging Black people was quite different than that of some of his peers. He rejected integration, saying it wasn't a worthwhile aim for their fight, and he also believed that Black people shouldn't surrender their right to self-defense against white people. While he wanted Black people to have the same rights as white people, he felt Black people shouldn't strive to be just like white people. Instead, he believed Black people should have and celebrate their own culture.

These beliefs were rooted in his identity as a member of the Nation of Islam, which is a Black nationalist organization. After he broke away from the Nation of Islam near the end of his life, his stance on certain aspects of the civil rights movement changed, and he became less confrontational toward King and the movement as a whole.

On February 21, 1965, Malcolm X was assassinated while giving a speech in New York City for the Organization of Afro-American Unity. The three men who were accused of murdering him were members of the Nation of Islam, which Malcolm X had left a year prior. One man was caught while trying to flee and confessed to his murder. However, the other two convictions ended up in a long miscarriage of justice that carried on up to 2021.

The convictions were reviewed in 2020, stating that the accused were wrongly convicted. In early 2021, Malcolm X's daughters wanted the investigation reopened due to new evidence of a deathbed letter from someone who was a policeman in 1965. The letter alleged that the New York police and Federal Bureau of Investigation (FBI) conspired in the murder.

pastor named Martin Luther King Jr. as its president. A year later, the MIA changed its name to the Southern Christian Leadership Conference (SCLC).

Malcolm X was a big influence during the civil rights movement. He traveled the globe, sharing the importance of fighting for equality and justice while also preserving Black culture.

The SCLC's primary goal was to desegregate cities through nonviolent resistance. On January 7, 1957, King stated that the SCLC was created out of a need to dig deeper into the struggle

In late 1963, King met with President Lyndon B. Johnson in the White House. The two worked together to create civil rights legislation.

FAST FACT

MANY OF KING'S IDEAS FOR NONVIOLENCE WERE BASED ON THE TEACHINGS OF MAHATMA GANDHI. BY FOCUSING ON PEACEFUL METHODS OF PROTEST, THE VIOLENT RESPONSES FROM WHITE PEOPLE WERE MORE OBVIOUS. WHEN AMERICANS SAW POLICE USING PRESSURIZED WATER JETS AND POLICE DOGS ON PEACEFUL PROTESTERS, IT CREATED OUTRAGE.

for civil rights and to do so with nonviolence.

King quickly became the main face of the civil rights movement. His peaceful protests and powerful speeches earned him the Nobel Peace Prize in 1964.

Along with making some of the most iconic speeches in the history of public speaking, King played a big role in many other parts of the civil rights movement. He attended sit-ins, he organized huge marches, he spoke directly with presidents, and he was put in jail more than once. At an Emancipation Day Rally with the NAACP in 1957, King reminded people that freedom was worth going to jail for as well as losing a job for and even dying for.

King's peaceful marches were modeled after those done by Mahatma Gandhi, shown in the top photograph. However, the two men never met.

HOW YOU SEE HISTORY

1. What did Rosa Parks mean when she said she was tired of giving in to discriminatory laws and demands? What role did that play in her following actions?
2. Why was the boycott of Montgomery's buses so successful?
3. How did Malcolm X look at civil rights differently than other activists? Do you think his perspective was valid?

CHAPTER FOUR

MARCHING FOR JUSTICE

The end of segregation was a major goal for the civil rights movement, and in many ways, it started with the end of school segregation.

The end of school segregation was a major victory for the movement, but the process of integration wasn't always easy, especially for the Black students who had to enter a new environment, where not everyone would be welcoming or accepting.

This is the situation Richard found himself in at the end of his time in high school. His experiences with integration shine a light on the process, including the groups who had the most difficulty accepting Black students in formerly all-white spaces.

ACCEPTANCE . . . FROM SOME

Richard was in high school when integration was occurring across the nation. He recalled the transition from all-Black schools to integrated ones in an interview:

I went to a segregated school for the first nine years. I was active in sports ... extracurricular activities, marching band, glee club, those kinds of things. So when I went to the 10th grade that's when, for me, the schools

Scan this QR code to watch Richard share his experience of going through the process of school integration as a teenager.

With integration, Black and white students shared classrooms and other resources.

> *were integrated. So my last three years in high school, I went to an integrated school.*

Richard said that the white students he knew were not upset about integration. "The white kids, they were receptive," he explained. "The issues mainly were with the white teachers, basically."

He added, "The students were fine ... it was just the administrators and the teachers who were the ones who were the barriers for the most part."

His experience was not unusual. Many white teachers across the country quit rather than be put into a position of teaching Black students. Others stayed but treated their Black students poorly. Many teachers at this time had grown up during the time of legal segregation and some struggled to accept these changes.

MARCH ON WASHINGTON

While students such as Richard navigated the new world of integrated schools, the leaders of the civil rights movement also focused on equality in employment and other areas of life for adults. In the

The 1963 March on Washington for Jobs and Freedom brought more than 250,000 people to Washington and was the site of one of most powerful speeches in U.S. history.

process, they created a moment that captured the eyes, ears, and attention of the entire world.

For years, Martin Luther King Jr., A. Phillip Randolph, and other leaders in the NAACP and SCLC had talked about marching in Washington to further their causes of job equality and personal freedom. They wanted to make a statement by giving passionate speeches and by filling the streets with people willing to stand up for racial equality. They were tired of the ongoing issues of high Black unemployment, continued segregation in the South, and other types of **disenfranchisement** based on skin color.

Finally, on August 28, 1963, their dream became a reality. More than 250,000 people from across the country came to Washington, D.C., which was more than double what the organizers had expected. It was the largest gathering for civil rights at the time. A sea of people filled the grounds around the Lincoln Memorial as King went to the podium to deliver his famous “I Have a Dream” speech. He was the 10th and final speaker of the day.

As King began speaking, he referred to his notes. However, he detoured when Black gospel singer Mahalia Jackson, seated nearby, shouted for him to tell the crowd about his dream, referring to one of his most-used phrases about his dream for racial

At the end of his speech, Martin Luther King Jr. paused to wave at the audience as they cheered and clapped.

THE CHILDREN'S CRUSADE

Young people also continued to play a major role in the movement. As Richard said, "We knew that things weren't right ... When I grew up, things were separate—separate lunch counters, separate water fountains, restaurants ... And we knew that things weren't right." The voices of these young people were raised up as part of the civil rights movement. In fact, several months before the famous March on Washington, King and other activists were in Birmingham, which was one of the most defiant southern cities. These men were desperate to find a way to get through to people, and one of the SCLC's leaders had an idea: rely on children.

Popular Black teens from a number of local schools were **recruited** to persuade students to join in a protest. When it was time to march, more than 1,000 students ages 7 to 18 skipped school to hold picket signs and sing freedom songs in the streets. They were repeatedly reminded at their meetings at the 16th Street Baptist Church before the march that this was a nonviolent demonstration. Even if someone threatened them, they were not to fight back.

For almost a week, these students gathered and marched. Many were thrown in jail and chased by police dogs, while others were doused with huge jets of waters from firehoses. King told the children to lock their arms so that the pressure of the hoses wouldn't knock them over.

Four months after what became known as the Children's Crusade, a bomb exploded at the 16th Street Baptist Church in Birmingham, killing four Black girls, and injuring more than 20. The FBI searched for the bombers for months. It wasn't until 2000 that four Ku Klux Klan members were **convicted** and sentenced to life in prison.

FAST FACT

IN 1999, 137 SCHOLARS FROM A VARIETY OF UNIVERSITIES DECIDED THAT KING'S "I HAVE A DREAM" WAS THE BEST AMERICAN SPEECH OF THE 20TH CENTURY.

harmony. This made King stop, put his notes down, and speak directly from his heart.

Instead of being a four-minute speech as planned, King's revised speech was more than 16 minutes long. In it, he outlined the dreams he had for unity, brotherhood, and equality.

The images of teens in Birmingham being injured and threatened, as well as the aftermath of the bombing, were shown each night on the evening news and in the newspapers across the country and even around the world. The horror of it, awful as it was, helped encourage people to get involved with the civil rights movement and to fight racial injustices. Young people made a difference, but some argued that the price of social change was too steep.

This statue depicts a police officer with a police dog attacking a protester during the civil rights movement.

THE CIVIL RIGHTS ACT

The Children's Crusade, the March on Washington, and King's "I Have a Dream" speech all combined to have an impact on the U.S. government. President John F. Kennedy championed the first Civil Rights Act that would

FAST FACT

A SCULPTURE OF THREE GERMAN SHEPHERD POLICE DOGS REARING OUT OF STONE WALLS WAS CREATED BY ARTIST JAMES DRAKE IN 1993 IN HONOR OF THE 1963 MARCH. IT IS FOUND ON FREEDOM WALK IN KELLY INGRAM PARK IN BIRMINGHAM.

On July 2, 1964, President Johnson signed the Civil Rights Act, surrounded by other political leaders and Martin Luther King Jr.

FAST FACT

ONE YEAR AFTER THE CIVIL RIGHTS ACT WAS PASSED, PRESIDENT JOHNSON SIGNED THE VOTING RIGHTS ACT OF 1965. IT WAS CREATED TO SECURE THE RIGHT TO VOTE FOR ALL RACIAL MINORITIES. IT WAS LATER AMENDED IN 1970, 1975, 1982, 1992, AND 2006 TO EXPAND ITS PROTECTIONS.

prohibit discrimination in public places and make it illegal to allow skin color play a role in employment. However, before he could sign the act, he was assassinated on November 22, 1963. Kennedy's vice president, who became president after the assassination, Lyndon B. Johnson, took up the cause and signed the act into law in 1964.

SELMA TO MONTGOMERY

In 1965, the next major moment of the civil rights movement took place: the marches from Selma to Montgomery in Alabama. At 54 miles (87 km) long, the route of the marches went from the city of Selma, Alabama, to Montgomery, Alabama. Approximately 600 protesters walked for three days, including John Lewis. When they reached the Edmund Pettus Bridge, they were met with state troopers armed with **billy clubs**, tear gas, and whips. Many were severely injured, including John Lewis. They had no choice but to return to Selma. However, the moment was immortalized as cameras clicked and rolled and images were captured and then shared on the national news. People across the country were shocked at the violence they saw.

President Johnson then went on television to show support for the Selma protesters, stating that it wasn't a problem of the North, South, or Black people, but was instead an American problem.

The marches from Selma showed people all around the world what was being done to Black people in the South and inspired many to join in local protests.

On Bloody Sunday, officers used billy clubs on unarmed protestors, as well as tear gas.

FAST FACT

MARCH 7, 1965, CAME TO BE KNOWN AS "BLOODY SUNDAY." AS HUNDREDS OF MARCHERS CROSSED THE EDMUND PETTUS BRIDGE, STATE TROOPERS BEAT MANY OF THEM AND SPRAYED THEM WITH TEAR GAS.

A week later, 2,000 protesters set out for Montgomery again, but this time they were escorted by U.S. Army troops. Three days later, they arrived at the Montgomery courthouse, where almost 50,000 people were waiting to support them. Huge steps had been made with these marches, but a huge loss was just around the corner.

HOW YOU SEE HISTORY

1. Was it appropriate for organizers to involve children in the protests? Why or why not?
2. Why do you think it took so long for the FBI to find and convict the men who attacked the 16th Street Baptist Church?
3. Why did catching the police brutality on camera change Americans' attitudes?

CHAPTER FIVE

PROGRESS AND PAIN

As the civil rights movement continued through the 1960s, moments of pain and progress continued to occur side by side. In some cases, the moments of pain were particularly challenging and bloody, as riots swept the country and major figures in the movement were assassinated.

One of the most painful moments in the history of the movement occurred when Dr. Martin Luther King Jr., was killed. His death impacted people around the country, including Larry, whose memories of the traumatic event have stayed with him since his teenage years.

THE LONG, HOT SUMMER

As the second half of the 1960s went on, the threat of violence seemed to be everywhere. The summer of 1967 was a difficult one for many Black people in the United States. It came to be called the "Long, Hot Summer" and it was full of violence and anger. Throughout the nation, riots erupted as Black citizens clashed with white police and military officers. According to a study published in *The Journal of Economic History*, more than 150 riots exploded

Scan this QR code to watch former New York Giants football player Larry Mallory share his memories about the assassination of Martin Luther King Jr.

Race riots like the one in Newark left cities tense, divided, and damaged.

> **FAST FACT**
>
> THE PROPERTY DAMAGE DONE IN NEWARK IN 1967 WAS VALUED AT $143 MILLION. DETROIT'S TOTALED MORE THAN $400 MILLION.

in U.S. cities, resulting in 83 deaths and 17,000 arrests.

The worst of the riots occurred in Newark, New Jersey, and Detroit, Michigan. Many people died, thousands were arrested, and countless buildings were damaged or destroyed. In a speech at Stanford University, Martin Luther King Jr. spoke about the cities being like powder kegs. All of the disappointment, desperation, despair, and bitterness in the Black communities was already there, about to explode into the riots.

A STAGGERING LOSS

In early 1968, the civil rights movement suffered a major blow. Memphis, Tennessee, was coping with a city-wide strike of its sanitation workers. Two of them had been killed by a malfunctioning garbage truck, and the workers were demanding a union that could help with improved safety standards.

To show his support for their cause, Martin Luther King Jr. came to Memphis to give a speech. While standing on the balcony of his

President Johnson confers with a variety of leaders, including J. Edgar Hoover, and Secretary of the Army Stanley Resor on what to do about the 1967 race riots.

hotel room before heading to dinner, King was shot in the neck by a sniper in a nearby boarding house. The shooter was James Earl Ray, a criminal and escaped convict. King died in the hospital an hour later. He was only 39 years old.

As the news spread, riots broke out in more than 100 cities. Thousands were injured, and far more were arrested.

Larry was in high school in Memphis at the time of the shooting. In an interview, he described the traumatic event and why it affected him so strongly: "I can ... remember more specifics around that event than ... other events ... because it was like I was in it. And I was a young person."

FAST FACT

AUTHOR AND ACTIVIST JAMES BALDWIN WROTE SEVERAL BOOKS AND PLAYS THAT FOCUSED ON RACE IN AMERICA. HIS WORKS ADDRESSED RACE RELATIONS WITH ANGER AND COMPLEXITY, MAKING HIM ONE OF THE MOST IMPORTANT VOICES OF THE 20TH CENTURY.

He also described the aftermath of the assassination on the Black community in Memphis: "The onslaught of the military and the police into our neighborhoods had an impact on me for a long time.

During the sanitation strike, the streets filled up with garbage, as there was no one to come by and remove it.

The power of control that was forced on us at that time touched everybody in my community."

President Johnson declared a state of emergency after the assassination and sent 4,000 National Guardsmen to Memphis. The search for King's killer was long and difficult. Ray managed to leave the

The riots in Washington, D.C., were huge and many people were hurt.

THE CHALLENGE OF MISCEGENATION

Richard Loving and Mildred Jeter were in love and planned to get married in their hometown of Central Point, Virginia. Unfortunately, their marriage was deemed illegal in their state under the Racial Integrity Act, which said that **miscegenation** would challenge racial integrity. Marriages between different races mustn't be allowed.

The couple went to Washington, D.C., to get married, but, when they returned to Virginia they were arrested and told to leave Virginia for 25 years or go to prison. The Lovings chose to leave Virginia.

The couple tried to make a home in Washington, D.C., but they never felt truly at home. They would periodically defy the court order to return to Virginia and see family. Because they weren't allowed to return together, they would have to take certain precautions to not be seen together. For example, Richard would not leave the house where they were staying in Virginia.

Richard Loving, a white man, and Mildred Jeter, a Black and Native American woman, were high school sweethearts who had to fight for years to preserve their marriage.

While the couple was struggling, the civil rights movement was happening, and the couple was inspired by the activism they saw. In 1964, Mildred contacted Attorney General Robert F. Kennedy, who told her to contact the American Civil Liberties Union (ACLU). Lawyers at the ACLU eagerly took the case, which made its way to the Supreme Court. In 1967, the judges decided that it was unconstitutional to ban interracial marriages.

FAST FACT

THE RACIAL INTEGRITY ACT OF 1924 HAD THE "ONE DROP RULE." IT DEFINED A WHITE PERSON AS SOMEONE WITH NO TRACE OF BLOOD FROM ANY RACE OTHER THAN WHITE. IF THERE WAS A SINGLE DROP OF BLOOD THAT WAS NOT WHITE, THE PERSON WAS CONSIDERED BLACK.

FAST FACT

THE FBI'S MANHUNT TO FIND RAY WAS THE BIGGEST TO DATE IN ITS HISTORY. IT INVOLVED 3,500 INVESTIGATORS AND COST MORE THAN $2 MILLION.

WANTED BY THE FBI

CIVIL RIGHTS - CONSPIRACY
INTERSTATE FLIGHT - ROBBERY

JAMES EARL RAY

FBI No. 405,942 G

Photographs taken 1960

Photograph taken 1968
(eyes drawn by artist)

Aliases: Eric Starvo Galt, W. C. Herron, Harvey Lowmyer, James McBride, James O'Conner, James Walton, James Walyon, John Willard, "Jim,"

DESCRIPTION

Age: 40, born March 10, 1928, at Quincy or Alton, Illinois (not supported by birth records)
Height: 5' 10"
Weight: 163 to 174 pounds
Build: Medium
Hair: Brown, possibly cut short
Eyes: Blue
Complexion: Medium
Race: White
Nationality: American
Occupations: Baker, color matcher, laborer
Scars and Marks: Small scar on center of forehead and small scar on palm of right hand
Remarks: Noticeably protruding left ear; reportedly is a lone wolf; allegedly attended dance instruction school; has reportedly completed course in bartending.
Fingerprint Classification: 16 M 9 U 000 12
M 4 W I0I

CRIMINAL RECORD

Ray has been convicted of burglary, robbery, forging U. S. Postal Money Orders, armed robbery, and operating motor vehicle without owner's consent.

CAUTION

RAY IS SOUGHT IN CONNECTION WITH A MURDER WHEREIN THE VICTIM WAS SHOT. CONSIDER ARMED AND EXTREMELY DANGEROUS.

A Federal warrant was issued on April 17, 1968, at Birmingham, Alabama, charging Ray as Eric Starvo Galt with conspiring to interfere with a Constitutional Right of a citizen (Title 18, U. S. Code, Section 241). A Federal warrant was also issued on July 20, 1967, at Jefferson City, Missouri, charging Ray with Interstate Flight to Avoid Confinement for the crime of Robbery (Title 18, U. S. Code, Section 1073).

IF YOU HAVE ANY INFORMATION CONCERNING THIS PERSON, PLEASE NOTIFY ME OR CONTACT YOUR LOCAL FBI OFFICE. TELEPHONE NUMBERS AND ADDRESSES OF ALL FBI OFFICES LISTED ON BACK.

J. Edgar Hoover
DIRECTOR
FEDERAL BUREAU OF INVESTIGATION
UNITED STATES DEPARTMENT OF JUSTICE
WASHINGTON, D. C. 20535
TELEPHONE, NATIONAL 8-7117

Wanted Flyer 442-A
April 19, 1968

The FBI immediately issued a wanted poster for James Earl Ray.

In April 1968, President Johnson signed the Civil Rights Act of 1968, which included the Fair Housing Act.

country, and it took until July to track him down. When his lawyers told him that there was absolutely no chance of acquittal, Ray finally pled guilty to the murder and was sentenced to 99 years in prison. During those years, he tried to escape twice and then, in April 1998, three decades after he killed King, Ray died from kidney and liver disease.

FAST FACT

THE FAIR HOUSING ACT PROHIBITED DISCRIMINATION BASED ON RACE, RELIGION, NATIONAL ORIGIN, OR SEX IN THE SALE, RENTAL, AND FINANCING OF HOUSING. IT WAS PASSED IN APRIL 1968, FUELED IN LARGE PART BY THE ASSASSINATION OF MARTIN LUTHER KING JR. TWENTY YEARS LATER, CONGRESS PASSED THE FAIR HOUSING AMENDMENTS ACT, EXPANDING THE LAW TO PROHIBIT DISCRIMINATION BASED ON DISABILITY OR FAMILY STATUS.

BLACK LIVES MATTER, THEN AND NOW

The civil rights movement is considered, by many historians, to have ended in 1968 with the assassination of Martin Luther King Jr. Others strongly disagree, arguing that the country's policies, attitudes, and actions related to racial inequality are far from fixed.

In 2013, a new chapter in the fight for civil rights began with to formation of a group known as Black Lives Matter (BLM). The organization's goals were familiar ones: ending white supremacy and systemic racism, stopping police brutality, and giving all races full access to resources. These are goals that would sound very familiar to the heroes of the civil rights movement, like Rosa Parks and Martin Luther King Jr.

Like their predecessors, the people involved with BLM focus on protests and marches, policy changes, and community building. BLM has become one of the largest and most active social justice movements in the world. In 2023, according to the Pew Research Center, 51 percent of Americans supported BLM.

FAST FACT

IN 1983, PRESIDENT RONALD REAGAN SIGNED LEGISLATION CREATING AN OFFICIAL MARTIN LUTHER KING JR. DAY TO HONOR THE WORK THE ICON DID FOR THE CIVIL RIGHTS MOVEMENT. IT WAS FIRST CELEBRATED ON JANUARY 20, 1986, TO BE CLOSE TO KING'S BIRTHDAY.

The Black Lives Matter movement began in 2013 and rose to a place of national attention in 2020.

As time has passed, the civil rights movement has evolved and adapted to deal with endless changes. And for as many steps as it has taken forward, there are still more to take. As Americans continue to grapple with the concepts of equality and justice for all, looking back at the history of this movement reminds them that everyone has the ability to take a look at the world around them and stand up for what is right.

FAST FACT

BLM FOCUSES ON NONVIOLENT PROTESTS. BETWEEN MAY AND JUNE, 2020, 89 PERCENT OF THEIR PROTESTS WERE PEACEFUL. AND BETWEEN JUNE AND SEPTEMBER 2020, MORE THAN 96 PERCENT OF THEIR DEMONSTRATIONS WERE NONVIOLENT.

HOW YOU SEE HISTORY

1. Do you agree with most historians that the civil rights movement ended in 1968? Why or why not?
2. What underlying conditions led to the "Long, Hot Summer" of 1967? Which do you think had the greatest impact, and why?
3. How are the goals of the Black Lives Matter movement similar to those of the 1960s civil rights movement? How are they different?

TIMELINE

VIOLENCE IN THE SOUTH: TIMELINE OF THE CIVIL RIGHTS MOVEMENT

1955: Emmett Till is killed.

FIGHTING SEGREGATION: TIMELINE OF THE CIVIL RIGHTS MOVEMENT

1909: The NAACP is established.

1954: The Supreme Court rules that segregation in public schools is unconstitutional.

1958: The Little Rock Nine are the first Black teenagers to attend a desegregated school in Arkansas.

1960: Ruby Bridges is the first Black student to attend her formerly all-white school in Louisiana.

THE FACES OF ACTIVISM: TIMELINE OF THE CIVIL RIGHTS MOVEMENT

1955: Rosa Parks refuses to give up her seat on a public bus in Montgomery, Alabama, starting a bus boycott.

1964: The first Civil Rights Act is signed.

1965: Malcolm X is assassinated.

MARCHING FOR JUSTICE: TIMELINE OF THE CIVIL RIGHTS MOVEMENT

1963: Students skip school to be part of the "Children's Crusade."

1965: The Selma to Montgomery marches are held.

PROGRESS AND PAIN: TIMELINE OF THE CIVIL RIGHTS MOVEMENT

1967: The "Long, Hot Summer" is full of race riots.

1968: Martin Luther King Jr. is assassinated in Memphis, Tennessee.

2013: Black Lives Matter is organized.

GLOSSARY

abolish: To end something.

acquit: To free someone from a charge.

activist: A person who campaigns for social change.

billy club: A short weapon used by police to hit people.

compliance: The following of a set of rules.

confrontation: When people challenge each other in an angry way.

convicted: To be found guilty of an offense.

disenfranchisement: When a group is deprived of a legal right or privilege.

evict: To force someone to move out of an apartment or off property using a legal process.

hate crime: A criminal offense against a person or group motivated by their race, gender, gender identity, disability, religion, or ethnicity.

mandate: An official command.

miscegenation: A marriage or other kind of romantic relationship between people of different races.

ratify: To approve a legally binding act.

recruit: To entice people to join something.

suffragist: Someone who advocates for the right to vote, often used to refer to a woman who fought for women's right to vote.

unconstitutional: Going against a country's constitution, or the document that formally establishes the laws and government of a place.

FOR MORE INFORMATION

BOOKS

Colbert, Brandy and Jeanne Theoharis. *The Rebellious Life of Mrs. Rosa Parks*. Boston, MA. Beacon Press, 2021.

Magoon, Kekla. *Revolution in Our Time: The Black Panther Party's Promise to the People*. Candlewick, 2021.

Mallory, Shadae. *The History of the Civil Rights Movement*. Emeryville, CA. Callistro Press, 2021.

Martin, Erica. *And We Rise: The Civil Rights Movement in Poems*. New York, NY. Viking Books for Young Readers, 2023.

Omokha, Rita. *Resist: How a Century of Young Black Activists Shaped America*. New York, NY. St. Martin's Press, 2024.

Yomtov, Nel. *1955: Exploring Civil Rights: The Movement*. New York, NY. Children's Press, 2022.

WEBSITES

Black Past

blackpast.org/

This extensive website is dedicated to providing accurate information about the history of Black people in the United States It lists timelines, events, biographies, and much more.

Civil Rights in America

www.nps.gov/subjects/civilrights/index.htm

The National Park Service offers news and events related to civil rights, as well as many videos and articles about important moments and people in the movement.

The Civil Rights Movement

www.loc.gov/classroom-materials/united-states-history-primary-source-timeline/post-war-united-states-1945-1968/civil-rights-movement/

The Library of Congress features a Primary Source Timeline of the key moments impacting the course of the civil rights movement. It offers links to additional sources, as well as documents.

Civil Rights Movement Archive

www.crmvet.org/

Through Duke University Libraries, this extensive archive includes speeches, videos, photographs, letters, poetry, and first person stories and memories of the movement.

Civil Rights Unit

online.kidsdiscover.com/unit/civil-rights

Kids Discover features eight articles on different elements of the civil rights movement, including Juneteenth and Heroes of the Movement.

INDEX

PHOTO CREDITS

Cover Martin Luther King Jr. addresses a crowd from the steps of the Lincoln Memorial, USMC-09611./Wikimedia Commons; p. 7 State Archives of Florida/Florida Memory/Alamy Photos; p. 9 Everett Collection/Shutterstock.com; p. 10 EmancipationPhoto/Wikimedia Commons; p. 11 13th Amendment Pg1of1 AC/Wikimedia Commons; p. 13 Sueddeutsche Zeitung Photo/Wikimedia Commons; p. 14 Emmett Till How She Sent Him and How She Got Him Back/Wikimedia Commons; p. 15 Tribune Content Agency LLC/Alamy Photos; pp. 16, 19, 20, 22, 24, 25, 39, 50 (bottom), 53 courtesy of the Library of Congress; p. 17 P20220329ES-0872 (52063715492)/Wikimedia Commons; p. 21 Civil Rights protesters and Woolworth's Sit-In, Durham, NC, 10 February 1960. From the N&O Negative Collection, State Archives of North Carolina, Raleigh, NC. Photos taken by The News & (24495308926)/Wikimedia Commons; p. 23 ZUMA Press, Inc./Alamy Photos; p. 27 Carlo Bollo/Alamy Photos; p. 29 Martin Luther King Jr. is welcomed with a kiss from his wife, Coretta Scott King, after leaving court in Montgomery, AL, on March 22, 1956/Wikimedia Commons; p. 30 Rosa Parks being fingerprinted by Deputy Sheriff D.H. Lackey after being arrested on February 22, 1956, during the Montgomery bus boycott/Wikimedia Commons; p. 31 Ian Dagnall/Alamy Photos; p. 32 Greyhound Bus Attack Anniston 5/Wikimedia Commons; p. 33 Martin Luther King, Jr./Wikimedia Commons; p. 35 Malcolm X 1962 press photo/Wikimedia Commons; p. 36 Martin Luther King, Jr. and Lyndon Johnson 3/Wikimedia Commons; p. 37 (top) Dinodia Photos/Alamy Photos; p. 37 (bottom) imageBROKER.com/Alamy Photos; p. 40 March on Washington for Jobs and Freedom, Martin Luther King, Jr. and Joachim Prinz 1963/Wikimedia Commons; p. 41 I Have a Dream in Color/Wikimedia Commons; p. 43 Jim West/Alamy Photos; p. 44 Lyndon Johnson signing Civil Rights Act, July 2, 1964/Wikimedia Commons; p. 45 Infobox collage for Selma to Montgomery marches/Wikimedia Commons; p. 46 Smith Archive/Alamy Photos; p. 48 Everett Collection Inc/Alamy Photos; p. 49 Meeting on Detroit riots Oval Office/Wikimedia Commons; p. 50 (top) Randy Duchaine/Alamy Photos; p. 51 Mildred and Richard Loving 1967 byUPI/Wikimedia Commons; p. 52 World History Archive/Alamy Photos; p. 54 Arnett Murry/Shutterstock.com.

ABOUT THE AUTHOR

TAMRA ORR is a full-time freelance author living in the Pacific Northwest. She has a degree in English and Secondary Education from Ball State University in Indiana. She has written hundreds of nonfiction/educational books for readers of all ages. Some of her titles include *People at the Center of the Civil Rights Movement*, as well a series that included *Frederick Douglass's Fourth of July Speech, Martin Luther King Jr.'s "I Have a Dream," Sojourner Truth's "Ain't I a Woman?,"* and *Barack Obama's Inaugural Address*. She and her husband, four children, two cats, and one grandchild are all constantly reading and learning about the world (except for those lazy cats!). As a former homeschooler, Orr taught her children about the civil rights movement and how it applies to the world today. Along with writing as a career, she is also a letter writer with pen friends from around the world. She designs her own cards and envelopes and almost always has either a pen or a book (sometimes both!) in her hand.